D0604641

For my family
Olivier

© 2001 Editions Parigramme / Compagnie parisienne du livre (Paris)

Monuments

that Tell Stories

of Paris

FROM THE ROMAN ARENA
TO THE GRANDE ARCHE AT LA DÉFENSE

TEXTS
Jean Daly

ILLUSTRATIONS
Olivier Audy

ENGLISH ADAPTATION
David W. Cox

PARIGRAMME
jeunesse

CONTENTS

Paris is a big city. But nobody would dream of walking around with a compass to find their way in the streets, avenues, or boulevards. It is far easier to get around by checking the landmarks – monuments that builders from Roman times to our own meant to be impressive, stunning, and unique.

Sometimes we walk past them without really seeing them or understanding how and why they were built. What a shame! Each one tells us about a period in history and how people lived in Paris long ago. Sometimes they tell about wars and revolutions!

Places of government, places of prayer, places to look at art, places to listen to music – monuments are places where things come to life. Some, like the Eiffel Tower, are famous the world over for their beauty and originality. Without them, Paris simply would not be Paris.

You must take time to understand these extraordinary constructions – listen to them tell their history, and let yourself dream of bygone days. In the ancient Roman arena, you can be a gladiator. In the Cluny Museum, you can be an aristocratic medieval lady. Outside Notre Dame Cathedral, squint hard at the roof and you might spot Quasimodo. One glance at the Paris Opera, and imagine you are a ballet dancer or an opera singer! Visit the oldest of Paris's monuments to get a peek at how Parisians lived centuries ago! Visit the most modern of Paris's monuments, like the Pompidou Center or La Villette, and rocket into the space age! Monuments are not mere decoration; they give the city its character and its force.

THE Roman ARENA

49, rue Monge, 5th arrondissement

CAGES

ARENA

The ancient Romans built this arena when Paris was called *Lutetia* and was a Roman city. This is why the French name for the place is *Les Arènes de Lutèce*. The Romans loved games, including the cruelest sorts. Here in the arena, gladiators fought lions and other gladiators with all kinds of weapons, and competed in thundering chariot races.

When the crowds had had enough of bloody games, the arena was easily transformed into an outdoor theater. Actors took the stage to delight audiences with comedies and tragedies.
Like any circus, the arena's oval form placed the audience around the center stage. The tiers of seats rose upwards. Only a part of them remains today.

Poor people crowded into the uppermost rows, while rich people had the best seats up front, right in the heat of the action. The arena was large enough to hold 17,000 spectators. In the wall under the tiers of seats, you can peer into three cages that held wild beasts.

SEATS

The Romans bathed more often than the Gauls (the native people). In every city that the Romans took over, they built baths on prime sites. Roman public baths were the size of our city swimming pools, but more complex. Ancient Paris had three baths, but only the one at Cluny remains today.

Going to the baths meant more than just a quick spray of water in a shower! The baths contained several rooms and pools.

Lovers of cleanliness always started by the hottest, the *caldarium*, where they worked up a sweat. Next, they stepped into the *tepidarium*, where they relaxed in lukewarm water in tubs that lined the walls. Finally, they finished off in the *frigidarium*, where they had a cool bath to perk up their skin and their spirits. While in all these rooms, they engaged in various exercises or relaxed in courtyards or in other rooms off to the sides of the pools of water.

The *frigidarium's* vaulted roof still holds up, a rarity for ancient Roman buildings. It is the only one still standing in France today.

THE Gallo-Roman BATHS

6, place Paul-Painlevé, 5th arrondissement

This small château (castle) was built at the end of the Middle Ages. Look closely at the outside walls, especially under the roof line, and you will see lots of sculpted animals staring back at you! There are squirrels, rabbits, dogs, and even lions!

This château was turned into a museum… a museum of the Middle Ages, naturally! Its collections include stained-glass windows from cathedrals, sculpture, armor, jewelry, household items, and numerous tapestries like the famous *Lady and the Unicorn*, which features lots of animals representing the five senses (sight, hearing, taste, smell, and touch).

The garden on the north side of the museum was recently replanted in medieval style. It contains medicinal plants used for curing illnesses in the Middle Ages. Off to one side of the garden is the Unicorn Woods inhabited by wild beasts that seem to have escaped from the famous tapestry.

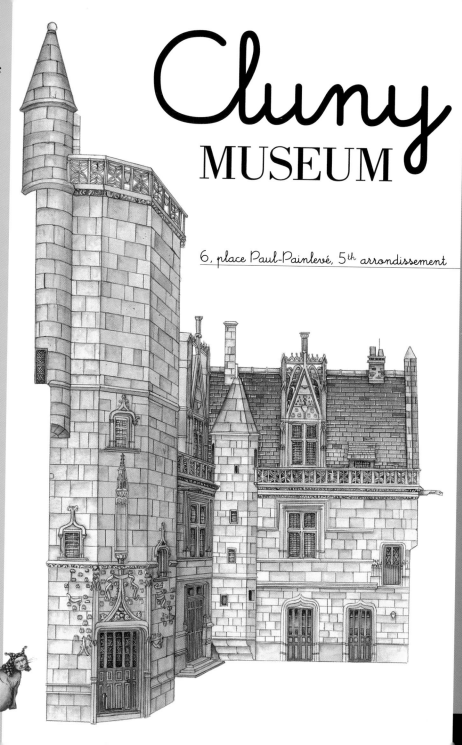

Cluny
MUSEUM

6, place Paul-Painlevé, 5th arrondissement

Notre-Dame
de Paris CATHEDRAL

This grandiose Paris cathedral was built in the Middle Ages on the island called Île-de-la-Cité, right in the heart of the city. Notre Dame looked slightly different from what you see today. First of all, you have to imagine that the stone façade (front of the building) was painted very much like an illuminated manuscript page. Secondly, you have to subtract the large esplanade (called a *parvis* in French) in front of the church. In the old days, it was a whole neighborhood of houses set along narrow streets.

Inside Notre Dame, everything is enormous. Architects of cathedrals wanted to show how great their faith in God was. This monument is 130 meters long (426 feet) and 48 meters wide (158 feet) : its towers rise 70 meters high (230 feet). To keep a large building like this from toppling over, medieval architects had to reinforce the sides with pillars called flying buttresses. On the façade are rows of statues representing kings mentioned in the Bible. Higher up is the circular stained-glass rose window, 13 meters (42 feet) in diameter. Looking at it from inside the cathedral, you might think it is made up of a veritable collection of precious multicolored gems.

On the esplanade in front of the cathedral is the zero milestone. All across the country, distances to Paris are measured from this point. So, if you go for a drive in the country and see a sign that says "Paris 160 km," you are exactly 160 kilometers (or 100 miles) from that marker in front of Notre Dame.

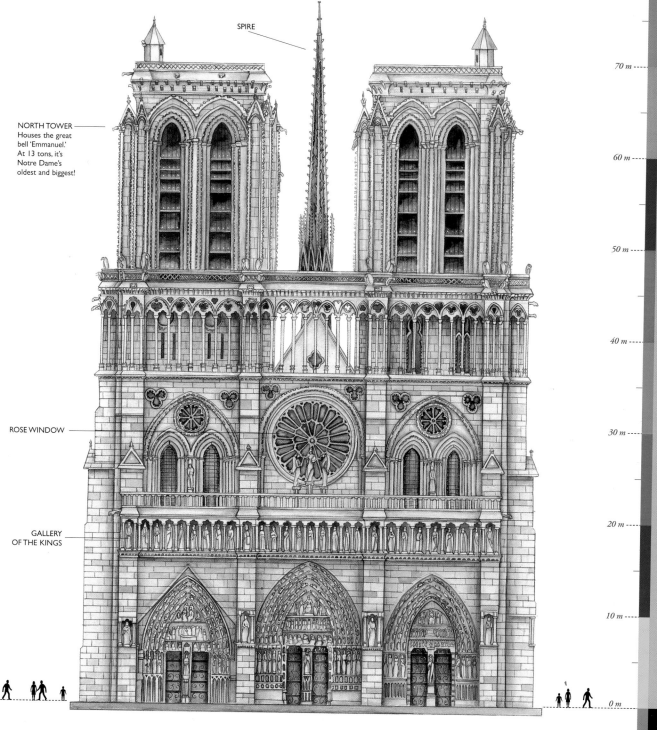

SPIRE

NORTH TOWER
Houses the great
bell 'Emmanuel.'
At 13 tons, it's
Notre Dame's
oldest and biggest!

ROSE WINDOW

GALLERY
OF THE KINGS

70 m

60 m

50 m

40 m

30 m

20 m

10 m

0 m

Long before it was a royal palace and a great museum, the Louvre was a fortified castle. Medieval King Philippe Auguste decided to protect Paris with a hefty wall so he could go on his crusades without worrying about enemy attacks. He also had a large keep built near the River Seine which was enclosed with ramparts. His treasure was placed in this castle keep. Later, King Charles V thought he could make the Louvre a pleasant residence if only the place were more comfortable. No sooner said than done! The Louvre expanded and became a fine royal palace with impressive reception halls, large windows, a library, a garden, and a zoo. This grand castle was entirely demolished by King François I because it was not at all to his liking. Therefore, very little remains of the Louvre as redesigned by King Charles V. You have to go down into the basement areas to discover the impressive stone foundations. Taking a stroll through the moat that surrounded the ramparts or a walk around the foundations of his castle keep is a real adventure, and full of mystery. Don't worry, it is not at all spooky. It's fun!

TOWER OF CHARLES V'S LIBRARY

KING AND QUEEN APARTMENTS

THE *Louvre* IN THE MIDDLE AGES

Place du Carrousel, 1ˢᵗ arrondissement. Beneath the Cour Carrée

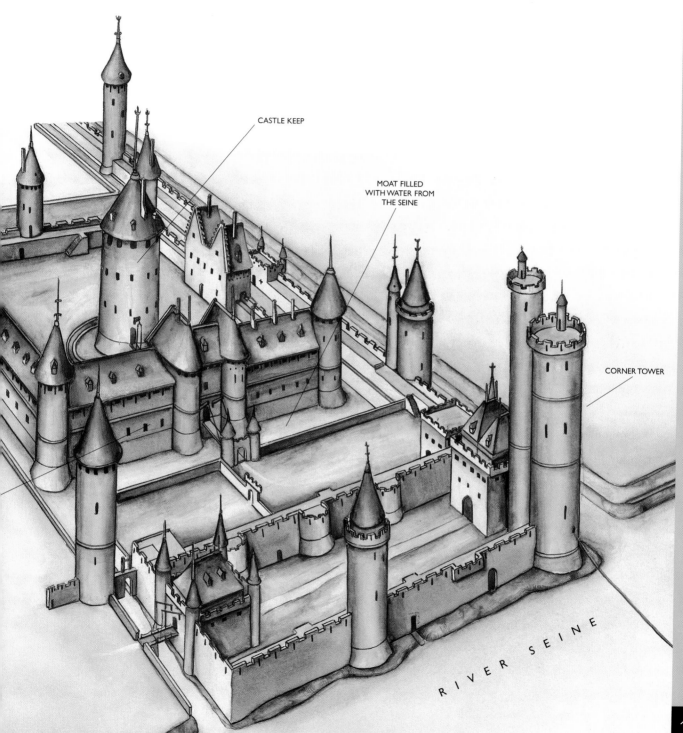

CASTLE KEEP

MOAT FILLED
WITH WATER FROM
THE SEINE

CORNER TOWER

R I V E R   S E I N E

King François I did not simply tear down the medieval towers. He built a whole new castle in a much more elegant style. It looked quite like those that were being built in the Loire River Valley. After him, other kings continued adding on to the Louvre. King Henri IV completed a long gallery along the riverside to connect the main residence with the Tuileries built for Queen Catherine de Medici. King Louis XIV finished the courtyard that François I had begun and added a grand façade with marble columns. But much more remained to be done. Emperors took over the job. Emperor Napoleon I ordered the construction of the wings along the Rue de Rivoli. Emperor Napoleon III finished the work on the Louvre, some 300 years after the renovation project had begun! Since then, the Louvre has become the world's largest museum! People from the world over come in droves to admire the collections of Egyptian, Greek, Roman, and Oriental antiquities, as well as the French, Italian, Dutch, and English paintings, the sculptures, and the treasures of the kings of France. With such vast collections, the museum needed more room. This is why the Louvre was completely renovated several years ago. Wide basement corridors were laid out, and the famous glass pyramid was set atop the new main entrance to the museum.

TURGOT PAVILION

RICHELIEU PAVILION

COLBERT PAVILION

SULLY PAVILION

THE LOUVRE PYRAMID

THE *Louvre* PALACE

DARU PAVILION

DENON PAVILION

MOLLIEN PAVILION

While on a crusade to Jerusalem, King Saint-Louis purchased a piece of wood that came from the cross that Jesus died upon.
The king also bought a piece of Jesus' crown of thorns. As he valued these objects more than any treasure of gold, he would not hear of shutting them up in some closet. No, no!
He required a magnificent chapel to house them. He ordered a chapel be built near his palace. And this is how the Sainte-Chapelle came to be.
Its magnificent stained-glass windows tell Bible stories and the life of Jesus very much in comic-book fashion.
Beside the Sainte-Chapelle stands the Conciergerie, also built in the Middle Ages by the grandson of King Saint-Louis. The four thick towers were slightly shorter than they are today, but otherwise looked very much like what you see today.
On the first tower, the only square one, is the oldest clock in Paris. It is over 400 years old!
The Conciergerie served as a prison for long time. The dark, dank, tiny cells were horrible places. Many famous people were locked up here, especially during the French Revolution. Queen Marie-Antoinette, the wife of King Louis XVI, was one of them.

THE *Sainte*

SPIRE

SAINTE-
CHAPELLE

PALACE
OF JUSTICE

Chapelle
AND THE CONCIERGERIE

4, boulevard du Palais and 1, quai de l'Horloge, 1ˢᵗ arrondissement

THE CLOCK
TOWER

CONCIERGERIE

CAESAR
TOWER

SILVER
TOWER

BONBEC
TOWER

L'HÔTEL
Carnavalet

Time for a French lesson! As in English, the word *"hôtel"* is of course a place where you can rent a room when you are away from home, but in French the word also means *"mansion"* (fancy homes for important people). Building mansions requires lots of land. Four hundred years ago there was plenty of open land in the Marais area. Hard to believe, but this was farmland back then. Aristocrats and rich families built magnificent mansions here. They turned it into a very chic neighborhood. In the fields in the area around Rue des Francs-Bourgeois rose up the first *hôtel* in Paris built between a courtyard, with a street entrance, and a garden where the owner of the little palace had the envious privilege of having it all to herself.

This home became a model for the other neighborhood mansions.

It belonged to the pretty young widow of a gentleman named Kernevenoy.

Naturally, such a complicated name got mangled.

It was not long before Parisians began calling it the "Carnavalet" mansion. Today, it is a museum devoted to the fascinating and rich history of the city of Paris – from prehistoric times to modern days.

WING
ON THE RUE DE SÉVIGNÉ

INSIDE COURTYARD

L'HÔTEL CARNAVALET

LE Pont-Neuf

On the River Seine, 1st and 6th arrondissements

In French, this name means "new bridge," and yet it is the oldest bridge in Paris! But when it was new, it was exceptional because it was the city's first truly sturdy bridge. The others had been destroyed by floods, fires, and other disasters. They had to be rebuilt several times. King Henri IV inaugurated the bridge nearly 400 years ago. You can see a statue of him on horseback off to the west side. This bridge was the first that was not lined with houses. At last, the River Seine was visible from a bridge! It also had sidewalks for pedestrian traffic (a real luxury back then!), with the added comfort of semi-circular recessed areas.

All this was so new, so innovative, that Parisians immediately became very fond of their new bridge, and took to strolling across it for pleasure. In the open air, merchants sold goods, dentists pulled teeth, jugglers and entertainers put on shows. And as unsuspecting passers-by gathered to watch, pickpockets plied their trade!

THE Bridges OF PARIS

Many other bridges were built after the Pont-Neuf. Today, Paris has a total of 36, each with its own history. Here are three that Parisians are particularly fond of.

The Passerelle des Arts is a footbridge. No cars or motorcycles allowed! It is very poetic and romantic. What a fabulous view it offers of the Île de la Cité!

The Pont Alexandre III is certainly one of the most gracious of Paris bridges with its garlands and gilded statues. It was built as an extension of the grand avenue of the Invalides esplanade. The bridge was named for Russia's czar as a tribute to the friendship between France and Russia in those days.

The Pont de l'Alma may not be the most elegant, but is famous for its statue of a soldier, called a Zouave. Parisians always check it to see how high the river is. You might hear them say, "Look! His feet are wet!" When they say, "Oh-oh! The Zouave is up to his knees in water," you can bet the river is high! In the great flood of 1910, the Zouave nearly had water up to his nose!

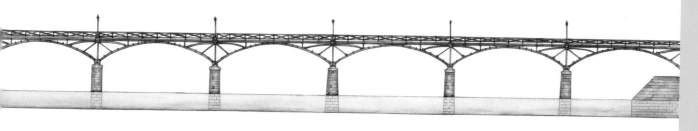

THE PASSERELLE DES ARTS

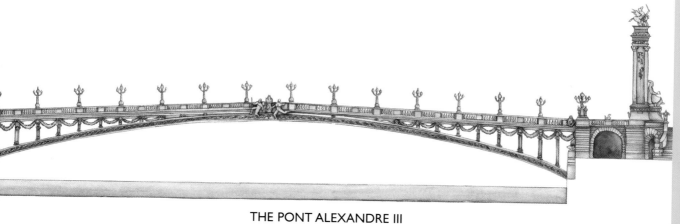

THE PONT ALEXANDRE III

THE STATUE OF THE ZOUAVE

THE PONT DE L'ALMA

LA PLACE DES VOSGES

4th arrondissement

This square was the first real public square designed in Paris. It was built on the site of a royal palace which was torn down and replaced by a horse market. King Henri IV wanted Paris to be the world's most beautiful city. He ordered that a royal place be built with all the houses in exactly the same architectural style. On the ground floor were covered arcades so that people could stroll from shop to shop and be protected from the weather.

The houses were all built in brick and stone, and topped with gray slate roofs. It quickly became a very fashionable place. Noble families held fabulous parties in their homes, and rich bourgeois families moved in. Later, famous actors, politicians, and writers found the Place des Vosges very much to their liking and moved in. The most famous writer who lived here was Victor Hugo, the author of *The Hunchback of Notre Dame*. By the way, why was this flat city square named after a mountain range in eastern France? Very simply because the people of the Vosges mountains were the first in France to pay their taxes 200 years ago. Naming this lovely square for their region was a way of thanking them for respecting their civic duty.

Luxembourg
PALACE

15, rue de Vaugirard, 6th arrondissement

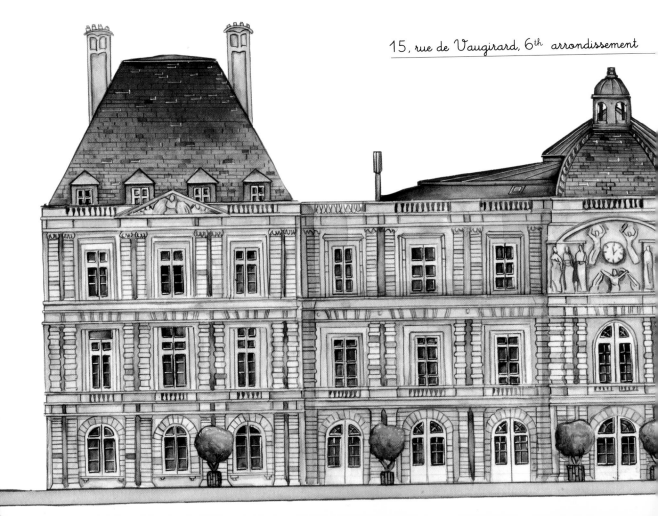

This beautiful palace was built for Marie de Medici, the wife of King Henri IV. Italian-born and bred, she missed the lovely garden homes of her homeland. She chose this site for her palace because it was then in the country. The construction and decoration of her new palace took fifteen long years. The wait was certainly worth it. Once finished, it was sublime! The greatest painters, the best tapestry-makers, the most skillful sculptors, and the most talented furniture-makers, worked to make each room an absolute marvel – fit for a queen! The queen's gardens, then larger than today, had paths, terraces, and fountains.

Unfortunately for her, Queen Marie de Medici did not live in her dream palace for very long. Sometimes queens have very complicated lives, and Marie was forced to leave Paris and even France only five years after settling into the Luxembourg Palace.

Today, no queen inhabits the palace. Senators meet here to pass laws. However, the garden is open to the public. Everybody can enjoy pleasant strolls in the greenery and admire the statues of the queens of France, or set pretty toy boats sailing across the ponds.

The Royal Palace was first called the Cardinal's Palace (*"Le Palais-Cardinal"* in French) because it was built for Cardinal Richelieu, a very important and very rich minister of King Louis XIII. Before he died, he gave his palace to the king, making it the *Palais-Royal*. Kings never lived in it, but royal family members and protégés did. Very little remains of the palace that Richelieu had built. Most of it burned in a fire. The rest of the estate was completely modified when one of the owners decided to build apartment buildings with boutiques and cafés on the ground floor, and collect the rent money!

Today, visitors enjoy strolling through the peaceful garden. Children enjoy playing leapfrog over the black and white striped columns of varying heights in the front courtyard.

LE
Palais-Royal

Place du Palais-Royal, 1ᵉʳ arrondissement.

LES Invalides

King Louis XIV established this veterans' institution. In those days, it was outside the city limits. It provided a place to live for soldiers wounded in wars and those who were too old for battle.
It was no small retirement home. Up to 5,000 soldiers (a veritable village-sized population) lived here.
The veterans' home had vast dormitories where they slept, a small hospital where they received medical care, mess halls where they had meals, and a church appropriately called the Soldiers' Church.
Although it was a beautiful church, it had one drawback from the king's point of view. It only had one entrance, and King Louis XIV wanted his own royal entrance. The "Sun King" required special treatment. "Yes, your Majesty! As You wish, Your Majesty!" A new church was built just behind the first. It was topped with a splendid gilded dome that shone like the sun.
The Sun King now had an entrance strictly reserved for him.
Many years later, it was under the dome of this church built for a king that the tomb of France's most famous emperor was placed: Napoleon I.

50 m

40 m

Columns
GALORE!

30 m

COLUMNS GALORE!

The obelisk on Place de la Concorde is 23 meters (75 1/2 feet) high. While it was erected on this site only some 150 years ago, in fact
it is the oldest column in the entire city. This obelisk was not made in France but in Egypt some 3,000 years ago for a pharaoh's temple.

Place de la Concorde, 8ᵗʰ arrondissement

20 m

The astrology column, 31 meters (101 feet) high, is all that remains of the palace built for Queen Catherine de Medici. It overlooks the gardens of the Forum des Halles. The Queen and her astrologer would climb up to the top of this column to try to read the future in the stars.

Rue de Viarmes, 1ˢᵗ arrondissement

10 m

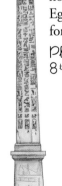

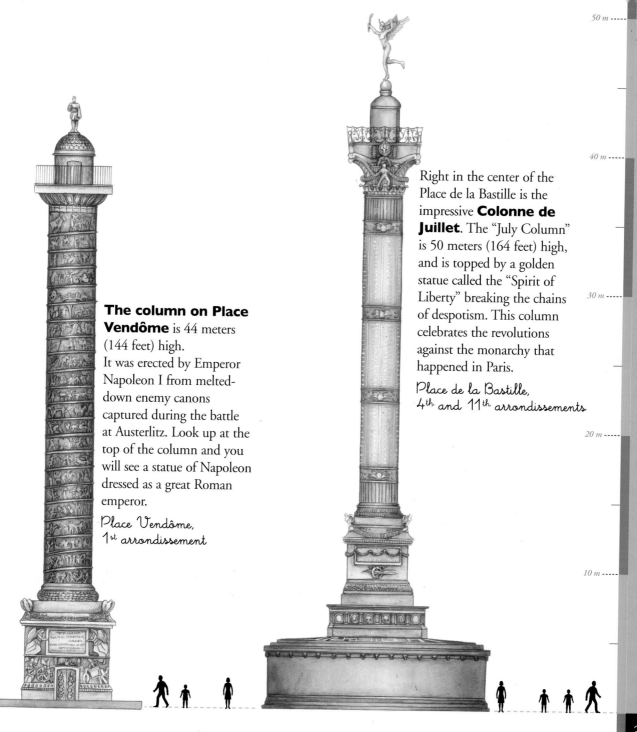

The column on Place Vendôme is 44 meters (144 feet) high.
It was erected by Emperor Napoleon I from melted-down enemy canons captured during the battle at Austerlitz. Look up at the top of the column and you will see a statue of Napoleon dressed as a great Roman emperor.

Place Vendôme,
1ˢᵗ arrondissement

Right in the center of the Place de la Bastille is the impressive **Colonne de Juillet**. The "July Column" is 50 meters (164 feet) high, and is topped by a golden statue called the "Spirit of Liberty" breaking the chains of despotism. This column celebrates the revolutions against the monarchy that happened in Paris.

Place de la Bastille,
4ᵗʰ and 11ᵗʰ arrondissements

50 m

40 m

30 m

20 m

10 m

50 m

40 m

30 m

20 m

10 m

0 m

THE *Arc* OF TRIUMPH

Place Charles-de-Gaulle, 8th arrondissement

An arc of triumph is a monument built to celebrate a military victory. Soldiers can parade through it to show their fellow citizens how mighty their army is and how brave their leaders are. This type of architectural structure is an ancient Roman invention, but many countries have them.

Paris has several arcs of triumph. The largest and most famous is on Place de l'Étoile (also called Place Charles-de-Gaulle). Napoleon I ordered it to celebrate his victory at Austerlitz. The construction turned out to be complicated, taking some thirty years, and Napoleon was long dead by the time it was completed. Standing 50 meters (164 feet) high, it holds the record as the highest of all arcs of triumph. On the right is a sculpture depicting the departure of volunteer troops to join the army while the country was in the midst of the great Revolution of 1789. It is known as *La Marseillaise* (which, by the way, is the title of France's national anthem).

The names of 150 military victories and over 650 officers are engraved on the ceiling of the vault. After the First World War, which claimed the lives of millions of soldiers, the tomb of the unknown soldier was placed beneath the Arc. He was a young man who fell in battle. Nobody knows his name. He was buried here to remind us of all the men who sacrificed their lives to defend France. A flame flickers over his tomb. Soldiers faithfully rekindle the memorial flame every day at 6:00 p.m.

THE SACRED HEART BASILICA:

Sacré-Cœur

Place du Parvis du Sacré-Cœur, 18th arrondissement

The *butte Montmartre* offers us a splendid view of all Paris. On a clear day, meaning when there is no smog, and if you have good eyesight, the panorama stretches for a good 30 miles. It was no easy task building the white basilica on Montmartre. It took 40 years! Building a church on a hilltop provided a gorgeous view, but a number of technical difficulties had to be overcome. Because the ground under this church had as many holes as Swiss cheese, engineers had to dig 80 meters down and pour tons and tons of concrete for the pillars that support the basilica.

Visitors are awestruck by how white Sacré-Cœur is. This is not because it is given a fresh coat of paint every week. A special type of stone was used which bleaches every time it rains. And as everyone knows, it rains quite a lot in Paris!

The Opéra
DE PARIS

Place de l'Opéra, 9th arrondissement

STATUE
OF MUSIC

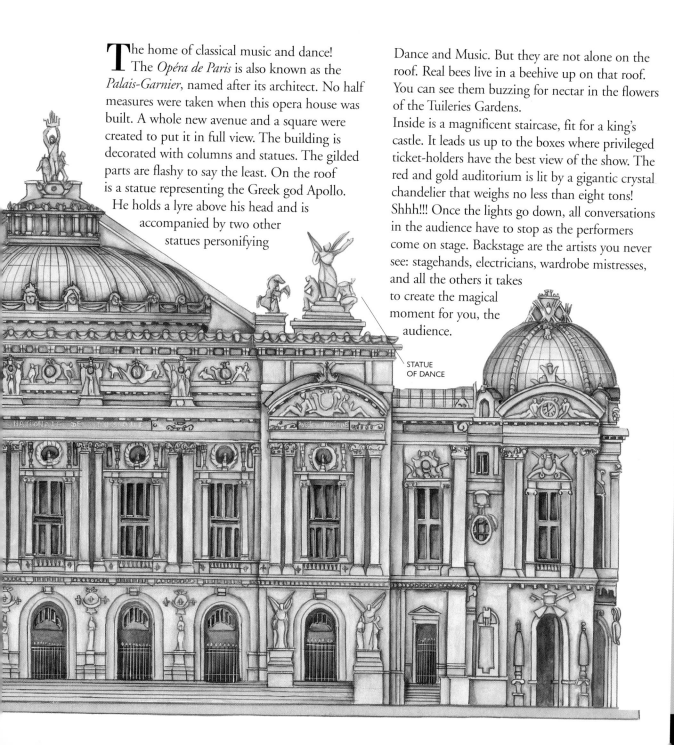

The home of classical music and dance! The *Opéra de Paris* is also known as the *Palais-Garnier*, named after its architect. No half measures were taken when this opera house was built. A whole new avenue and a square were created to put it in full view. The building is decorated with columns and statues. The gilded parts are flashy to say the least. On the roof is a statue representing the Greek god Apollo. He holds a lyre above his head and is accompanied by two other statues personifying

Dance and Music. But they are not alone on the roof. Real bees live in a beehive up on that roof. You can see them buzzing for nectar in the flowers of the Tuileries Gardens.

Inside is a magnificent staircase, fit for a king's castle. It leads us up to the boxes where privileged ticket-holders have the best view of the show. The red and gold auditorium is lit by a gigantic crystal chandelier that weighs no less than eight tons! Shhh!!! Once the lights go down, all conversations in the audience have to stop as the performers come on stage. Backstage are the artists you never see: stagehands, electricians, wardrobe mistresses, and all the others it takes to create the magical moment for you, the audience.

STATUE OF DANCE

Paris
CITY HALL

Place de l'Hôtel de Ville, 4th arrondissement

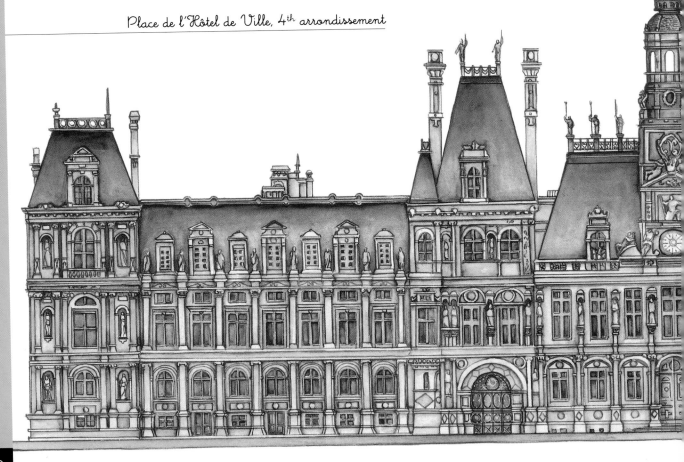

The mayor of Paris works here along with thousands of staff members. They keep the city running smoothly, and make sure that Paris is kept as pleasant as possible. While the building is not even 150 years old, it looks much older. Why? This is very simply because it is a copy of the Renaissance city hall, started under King François I and finished by King Henri IV.

Unfortunately, that building burned down. When city officials decided to rebuild, they voted on a copy of the Renaissance building.

On the same site, back in the Middle Ages, there was a building where important merchants met. Their leader was a sort of city mayor. On the square behind this building, festivities were held. But it was also where criminals were punished and subjected to awful tortures. Ugh!

320 m

280 m

240 m

200 m

THE

EIFFEL TOWER

The EIFFEL Tower

TELEVISION ANTENNA

3ʳᵈ LEVEL

The Eiffel Tower is the most famous of the monuments in Paris. It was built over 100 years ago by Gustave Eiffel, and that is how it got its name. He wanted to beat the world's record for the highest monument by erecting a 1,000-foot tower. The highest cathedrals of the time did not rise even half that height. Gustave Eiffel had a brilliant idea: his tower would be iron, much lighter than anything built in stone, and would not risk toppling under its own weight. It barely took two years to erect – quite an accomplishment!

He prefabricated whole portions of it in his workshops, then fitted the pieces together like a toy construction set on the banks of the River Seine. It is now the most visited monument in Europe, but the Eiffel Tower had plenty of critics in its day. Not everybody liked it. Some thought it was plain ugly and nastily called it the "Awful Tower." There were several plans to tear it down. But it is still standing, and has even grown.

2ⁿᵈ LEVEL

With the television antennas on it, the "Iron Lady" stands over 320.75 meters high (1,052 feet). Today, it is not the highest building in the world, even the now-dwarfed (though very famous) Empire State Building in New York City beats it, standing 448 meters (1,472 feet). What difference does it make? Since the year 2000, the Tower has been shimmering gorgeously, lighting up Paris nights, more beautiful than ever!

1ˢᵗ LEVEL

THE Orsay MUSEUM

1, rue de Bellechasse, 7th arrondissement

Before becoming a great art museum, this beautiful building was a train station. It was quite a fine one in its day! Built in 1900, it was the most graceful of all Paris train stations, but it was also the cleanest. Only new electric locomotives could pull in. Bye-bye to those old, smoking, soot-spewing locomotives!

Beautiful does not always mean practical, however. It soon proved to be too small for the increasingly longer trains being developed. The station was closed, and nobody knew what to do with it… until one day someone had the fabulous idea of turning it into a museum. On display are sculpture and paintings created 100 or even

150 years ago, plus models of the monuments of Paris! At Orsay you can see lots of impressionist paintings. They are called impressionist because the artists dabbed colors onto the canvases to give only impressions of what they saw in their subjects: trains, sail boats, flags, horses, and even pretty ballerinas from the Opera.

ESPLANADE

LE Palais DE CHAILLOT

Place du Trocadéro, 16th arrondissement

Many Paris monuments were built for universal exhibitions which attracted people from all over the world. Such was the case of this palace, built in 1937. The architects had to solve some mighty tough problems. With the Eiffel Tower (built 48 years earlier for the 1889 Universal Exhibition) on the opposite bank of the River Seine, the question was how to design something that would not appear ridiculously tiny next to something so big. The solution was fairly simple: space! They planned plenty of space between the two, and laid out a vast esplanade (which roller skaters particularly appreciate today). The fabulous view of the Eiffel Tower became one of the best assets of the palace. Gardens were planted on the steeply sloping riverbank. The long descending fountain sprays cool refreshing water.

Children love splashing in the fountain on hot summer days!

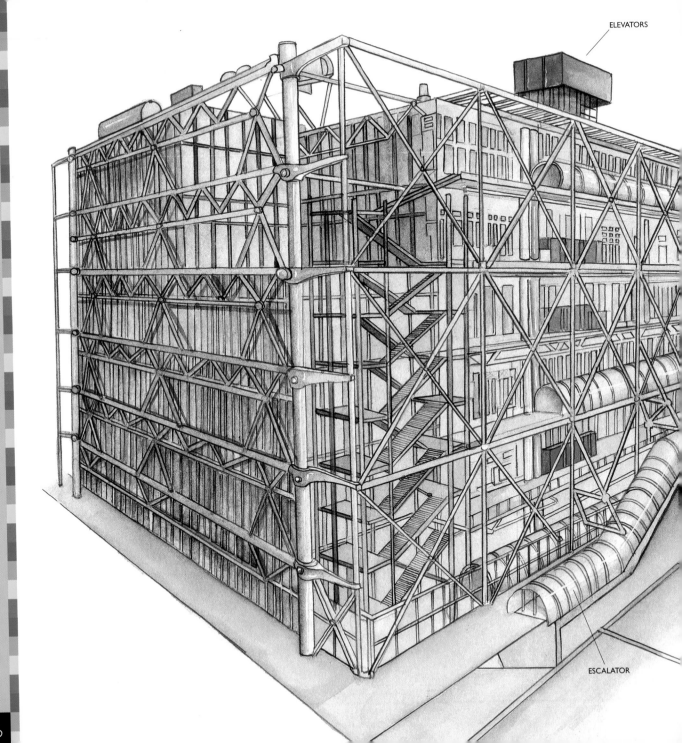

ELEVATORS

ESCALATOR

The GEORGES POMPIDOU Center

ESPLANADE

The Pompidou Center owes its name to a modern president of France who loved modern art. President Georges Pompidou commissioned the museum. It was built on a large empty space that was once a parking lot for trucks delivering meat, cheese, fruit, and vegetables into the Halles market place. Today, that market has been moved out to a suburb. The Pompidou Center is home to many cultural attractions. Besides its immense art museum, it boasts a wonderful library, concert halls, movie theaters, workshops for kids, and lots, lots more! This monument, and it certainly qualifies as one, is unlike any other you will ever see.

The architects deliberately pushed the steel tubes, air ducts, cables, elevators, and ceiling beams to the outside. Just for fun, they wanted to turn a building inside out! Each element was painted a specific color to be easily identifiable: yellow for electrical casings, green for water pipes, and blue for air ducts.

When you get off the escalator at the top floor, you are treated to a truly spectacular view of Paris.

THE CITY OF *Science* AND *Industry*

30, avenue Corentin-Cariou, 19th arrondissement

GÉODE

This colorful and ultra-modern museum is located within an amazing park with poetically-named theme gardens: the garden of mirrors, the fog garden, the bamboo garden, etc. And you won't want to miss sliding down the giant dragon's tongue.
The City of Science is full of life. Whether you are interested in airplanes, cinema, animals, how plants grow, the human body, or any other subject, you can be sure to find workshops and presentations to satisfy and stimulate your curiosity. There is something for every interest and every age.
You will also discover huge aquariums, models of airplanes, a greenhouse, a real submarine, a children's multimedia library, and a shiny silvery odd ball called the *Géode*. It has the world's largest hemispherical movie screen which wraps round the audience. Warning! The movies are so realistic and captivating, they can be scary! While watching a movie about marine life, you may forget you are snug as a bug in a cinema, and start wondering how you will ever swim out of there and away from those feisty sharks heading straight at you! Yikes!

ARGONAUT
SUBMARINE

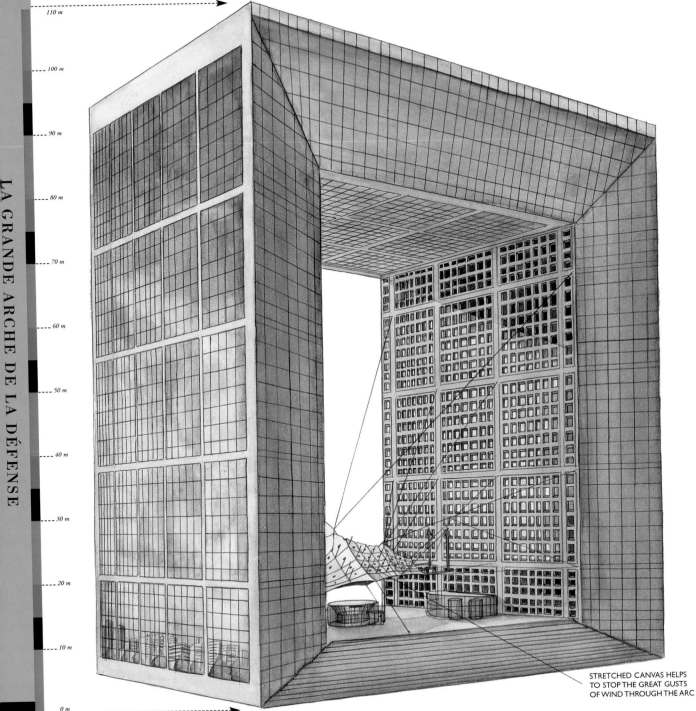

110 m

100 m

90 m

80 m

70 m

60 m

50 m

40 m

30 m

20 m

10 m

0 m

STRETCHED CANVAS HELPS
TO STOP THE GREAT GUSTS
OF WIND THROUGH THE ARC

LA Grande Arche
DE LA DÉFENSE

Parvis de la Défense, 92

"**G**rande" is the right word: 70 meters wide (230 feet) and 110 meters high (360 feet). It is twice the size of the Arc of Triumph. The Grande Arche does not celebrate any military victories. If anything, it celebrates a game of perspective started long ago, which consists of building different new monuments in Paris on the same straight line – kind of like somebody having fun with one gigantic ruler. Starting point: the Louvre's Cour Carrée, onwards through the new glass pyramid, straight through the Arc de Triomphe du Carrousel, then buzzing through the Egyptian obelisk on Place de la Concorde, zooming up the Champs-Élysées, through the center of the Arc of Triumph at Place de l'Étoile, and ending with the mammoth Grande Arche. Phew! What could possibly be next?

Anybody with a good eye will notice that the Grande Arche is slightly off kilter with the Arc of Triumph.

The architects had to cheat with the perspective. You would too if you had to build over all those subway tunnels and the underground parking areas. Every day, thousands of people swarm out of the subway and head up to their offices in the skyscrapers. La Défense is probably the only area of Paris that resembles an American city.

Versailles
AND ITS
CHÂTEAU

Place d'Armes, 78000 Versailles

King Louis XIV was only 23 years old when he started the construction of Versailles. The young monarch knew exactly what he wanted. He wanted to build the most beautiful château in the entire world – a château as grand as himself, the most powerful king on Earth. His grand design required that new marble quarries be opened. He created new factories to make the mirrors, tapestries, silk, and porcelain that would be used in the interior decoration. He put to work nearly 40,000 laborers. When the digging did not go fast enough, Louis XIV sent soldiers out to Versailles with shovels and pickaxes! His Majesty took particular interest in the gardens that his landscape architect, Le Nôtre, laid out to glorify him. The master gardener set out flower beds, groves, fountains, and artificial ponds. All this required phenomenal quantities of water, which simply were not available in Versailles. But where there is a will, there is a way! The king's engineers devised very sophisticated hydraulic works with miles and miles of underground pipes to bring water from nearby lakes, ponds, and the River Seine.

The king's bedchamber was in the heart of the château, at the crossroads of the axis formed by the waterworks and the sun's daily journey, thus putting the king at the center of the universe.

By the end of the reign of Louis XIV, the château and its grounds had attained absolute perfection – the culmination of a 50-year-old dream that belonged to a young man who held (nearly) unlimited powers over nature and people.

Conception graphique Isabelle Chemin
Photogravure Alésia Studio

Achevé d'imprimer en RAE en novembre 2010

Dépôt légal : octobre 2001
2-84096-251-9

Loi n° 49-956 du 16 juillet 1949 sur les publications destinées à la jeunesse